Measure It with Math!

MEASURING WEIGHT

Anne O'Daly

PowerKiDS press

Published in 2024 by The Rosen Publishing Group, Inc.
2544 Clinton Street, Buffalo, NY 14224

Portions of this work were originally authored by Chris Woodford and published as *Weight*.
All new material this edition authored by Anne O'Daly.

Children's Publisher: Anne O'Daly
Design Manager: Keith Davis
Picture Manager: Sophie Mortimer

Picture credits:
Key: t = top, tr = top right, b = bottom
Front Cover: Shutterstock: Cstleski tr, Four Oaks l, fotoslaz tl, Nuam Foto r.
Interior: iStock: sezer66 15, urbazon 14; NASA: ISS/expedition 68 5; Shutterstock: Evannovostro 9, fotolaz 28l, Four Oaks 26, Pradeep Gaurs 13, James Bloor Griffiths 16, Nut Korpsrisawar 17, Alekandr M 22, marvic 23, Beneda Miroslav 24, MatsB 11b, Pressmaster 4, Valentina Proskurina 11t, romakoma 20, Goran Safarek 1, 27, santypan 25, thieury 12,VladKK 19, Sharon Wills 8, WitR 10.

Cataloging-in-Publication Data

Names: O'Daly, Anne.
Title: Measuring weight / Anne O'Daly.
Description: New York : Powerkids Press, 2024. | Series: Measure it with math! | Includes glossary and index.
Identifiers: ISBN 9781642827941 (pbk.) | ISBN 9781642827958 (library bound) | ISBN 9781642827965 (ebook)
Subjects: LCSH: Weight (Physics)--Measurement--Juvenile literature. | Weights and measures--Juvenile literature. | Measurement--Juvenile literature. | Mathematics--Juvenile literature.
Classification: LCC QC90.6 O34 2024 | DDC 530.8'1--dc23

Manufactured in the United States of America
CPSIA Compliance Information: Batch #CSPK24. For further information contact Rosen Publishing at 1-800-237-9932.

Contents

What Is Weight?

Pick up a pencil. Then pick up a chair. The chair is heavier than the pencil. Heavy objects have more weight. Their weight is caused by gravity. Gravity is a force that pulls things toward Earth. Heavy things are pulled toward Earth more than light things are.

Mass and Weight

Things have weight because they have mass, but mass and weight are not the same. Mass is the amount of matter something is made from. A big truck has more mass than a car because it contains more metal. Because the truck has more mass, gravity pulls it to Earth more. So the truck weighs more than the car.

This weight lifter has to overcome the force of gravity to lift a heavy weight.

The mass of an object is always the same, wherever it is. But its weight can change depending on gravity.

Changing Gravity

Gravity changes in different places on Earth. The gravity at the top of a mountain is weaker than at the bottom. A car would weigh less at the top of a mountain than at the bottom. But its mass would be the same.

Astronauts on board the International Space Station weigh less than they do on Earth.

FLOATING IN SPACE

The International Space station travels around Earth about 200 miles (320 km) above it. At this height, gravity is about one-tenth weaker than on Earth. An astronaut who weighs 100 pounds (45 kg) on Earth would weigh about 90 pounds (40.8 kg) on the space station. Their mass would be the same.

FACT

Gravity on the moon is weaker than on Earth. Astronauts weigh six times less on the moon as they do on Earth.

History of Weights

People have been weighing things for thousands of years. Ancient people needed to know the weight of things when they were building or when they were exchanging food and other goods.

Ancient Romans needed to know about weights for their building projects.

WEIGH LIKE A ROMAN

The Romans invented a weighing machine called a steelyard. It looked like a seesaw. You hang the object you want to weigh on the hooks of the machine and move the weight along the arm until the arm balances. Then the object's weight is read from a scale on the arm.

Ancient Egypt

People who study history dig things out of the ground. They find items that show how people lived many years ago. They have found weights in graves in Egypt. The weights are more than 6,000 years old. Some of the weights are lumps of stone. Others are carved into shapes.

FACT

The Roman word for pound was libra. That is why we use "lb" as a short way of writing pounds.

Roman Weights

Two thousand years ago, the ancient Romans invented the weights we still use today—the ounce, pound, and ton.

Around 1800, people in France started to use a new system for measuring things. This is the metric system. Most countries, but not the United States, now use the metric system.

Imperial Weights

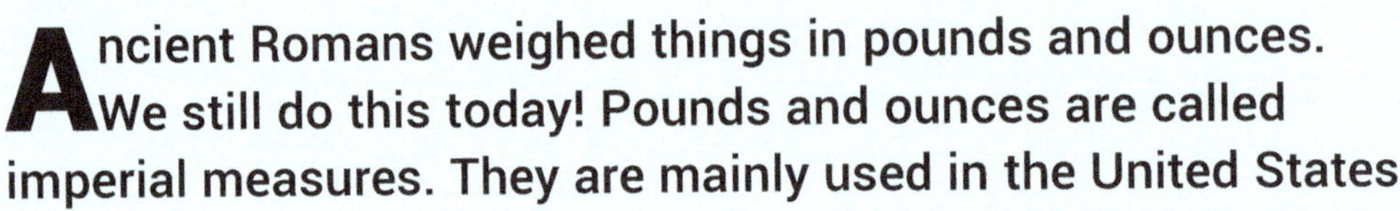

Ancient Romans weighed things in pounds and ounces. We still do this today! Pounds and ounces are called imperial measures. They are mainly used in the United States.

A pound is a small weight. An ordinary bag of table sugar weighs five pounds. An ounce is even smaller. People measure lighter things in ounces. There are 16 ounces in a pound. Two pencils weigh about 1 ounce.

Bigger and Heavier

People need bigger units to weigh heavier things. Heavy things like sacks of coal are sometimes measured in hundredweights. A hundredweight is the same as 100 pounds. A big sack of flour weighs about a hundredweight.

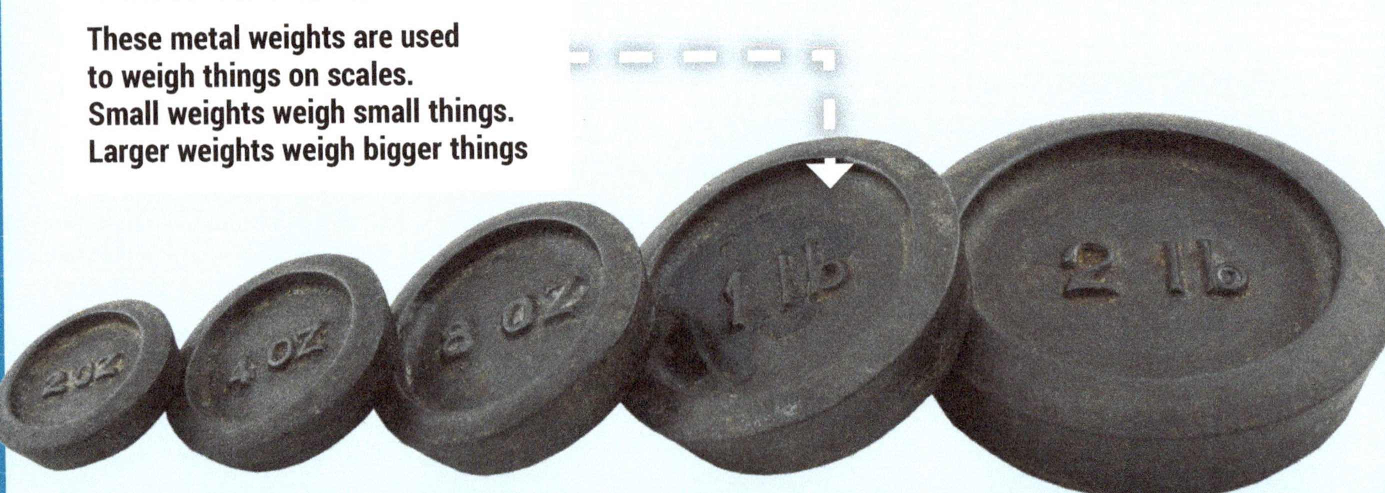

These metal weights are used to weigh things on scales. Small weights weigh small things. Larger weights weigh bigger things

A small car weighs about a ton.

Heavier objects, like cars and trucks, are weighed in tons. A ton is sometimes called a short ton. It is the same as 2,000 pounds.

Units Matter

Ounces, pounds, and tons are units of weight. The unit tells us how big something is. Three ounces is a smaller weight than three pounds. Three tons is heavier than three pounds.

The number three means something different each time. The unit tells us what it means.

TRY THIS

Use scales or ask an adult to find the missing weights.

Pencil	? ounces
Book	? ounces
Bag of table sugar	? pounds
Bag of flour	? pounds
Baby	8 pounds
Child (you!)	? pounds
Large car	2 tons

Earth

600,000,000,000,000,000,000 tons = 600 quintillion tons

Measure with Metric

Most countries use the metric system for measuring. In the metric system, lengths are measured in centimeters and meters. Weight is measured in grams and kilograms. One kilogram weighs about as much as a big can of tomatoes. A kilogram is the same as 2.2 pounds.

There are bigger and smaller measures than kilograms in the metric system. The smallest metric weight most people use in everyday life is the gram (g). An ounce is the same as 28 grams, so a gram is a very small weight.

FACT

A paper clip weighs about 1 gram. There are 1,000 grams in 1 kilogram.

These weights go from 1 g (the smallest) to 2 kg (the largest).

A pineapple weighs about 1 kilogram.

Metric Tons

To measure really heavy weights in the metric system, people use metric tonnes. A metric tonne weighs 1,000 kilograms.

A full-grown walrus can weigh 1 tonne.

TRY THIS

IMPERIAL TO METRIC

1 ounce is the same as 28 grams

How many grams are there in 3 ounces?

16 ounces, or 1 pound, is the same as 454 grams, or 0.454 kilogram

How many grams are there in 5 pounds?

1 short ton is the same as 0.9 metric ton

METRIC TO IMPERIAL

1 gram is the same as 0.04 ounce

How many ounces are there in 6 grams?

1 kilogram is the same as 2.2 pounds

How many pounds are there in 10 kilograms?

1 metric ton is the same as 1.1 short tons

Answers on page 32.

Weighing Machines

The earliest weighing machines were balances. They are still used today. A balance has a beam that rests on something, a bit like a seesaw. A pan hangs from each end of the beam. To weigh an object, you put it on one pan. Then you put weights on the other pan. When the scales balance, the weight is the same on each side. If you count the weights, you know how much the object weighs.

The pans on either side are balanced. The fruit must weigh the same as the metal weight.

Weighing Candies

You can also put the weights on first. To measure 10 ounces of candies, for example, a shopkeeper puts 10 ounces of weights on one pan. Then they put candies on the other pan until the scales balance.

A shopkeeper weighs a box of sweets using a balance.

TRY THIS

People who work in banks often weigh coins rather than count them. Each coin weighs the same. By weighing the coins, the teller can figure out how many coins there are.

1 quarter weighs 0.2 ounce

1 nickel weighs 5 grams

If a bag of quarters weighs 12 ounces, how many quarters are there?

If a pile of nickels weighs 100 grams, how many nickels are there?

Answers on page 32.

Spring Balances

Have you ever baked a cake? You probably had to weigh the ingredients carefully using a kitchen scale. A kitchen scale is a spring balance. It has a single pan. There is a dial under the spring with numbers on it.

Lining Up

To use a weighing scale like this, you set the pointer so it lines up with the zero mark. Then, you put something on the pan to weigh it. The pan is pushed down, and the pointer moves. You can read the weight on the dial. Some kitchen scales show the weight on a digital screen.

This woman is weighing some flour. Ingredients have to be carefully measured to make a recipe work.

WEIGHBRIDGE

Trucks are weighed on a massive scale called a weighbridge. This is like a huge spring balance that is built into the road. The weighbridge weighs the truck when it is empty and when it is loaded. That shows how heavy the load is. An overloaded truck can damage roads. It can be harder to steer and take longer to stop.

A truck is weighed on a special scale to make sure it isn't too heavy.

Squashing the Spring

Scales like this are sometimes called spring balances because they have a spring inside. When you put a weight on the pan, it pushes downward. That squashes the spring.

The heavier the weight, the more the spring squashes. As the spring squashes, it moves the pointer around the dial or along the scale. When the weight is taken off again, the spring goes back to its old shape.

Light Weights

Have you ever held a feather in your hand? A feather is so light, you can hardly feel it. But light things have weight, just as heavy things do. A piece of paper does not weigh very much, but it still has weight. Light things do not weigh much, but people still need to weigh them.

Accurate Scales

People need accurate scales to weigh very light things. The scales have their own special units. Some jobs have their own measuring systems. Jewelers use a measuring system called troy weights. The units are ounces, pennyweights, and grains. There are 24 grains in a pennyweight. Twenty pennyweights make 1 troy ounce, and 12 troy ounces make 1 troy pound. Four troy pounds make 1 imperial pound.

A bee hummingbird weighs less than 2 grams. That's lighter than a dime coin.

Diamonds are weighed with special scales that use very small units.

Carats

A carat is a very light measurement of weight. One carat is the same as 200 milligrams. Diamonds are weighed in carats. A diamond that weighs 1 carat is about ¼ inch (6 millimeters) in diameter.

MILLIGRAMS

In the metric system, people weigh light things using milligrams (mg). There are 1,000 milligrams in 1 gram, so a milligram is a very light weight. A housefly's wing weighs about 1 milligram. So does a small snowflake.

FACT

A nanogram is one billionth of a gram! Scientists use it to measure tiny weights.

What Is Density?

Bigger objects usually weigh more than smaller ones. But that is not always true. Sometimes, what the object is made of can make a difference. A metal weight is often heavier than it looks. We cannot always tell how much something weighs just by looking at it.

Suppose we have a block of wood and a lump of metal that are exactly the same size. The metal weighs more than the wood. Metal has a higher density than wood. Density is a measure of how much matter something contains.

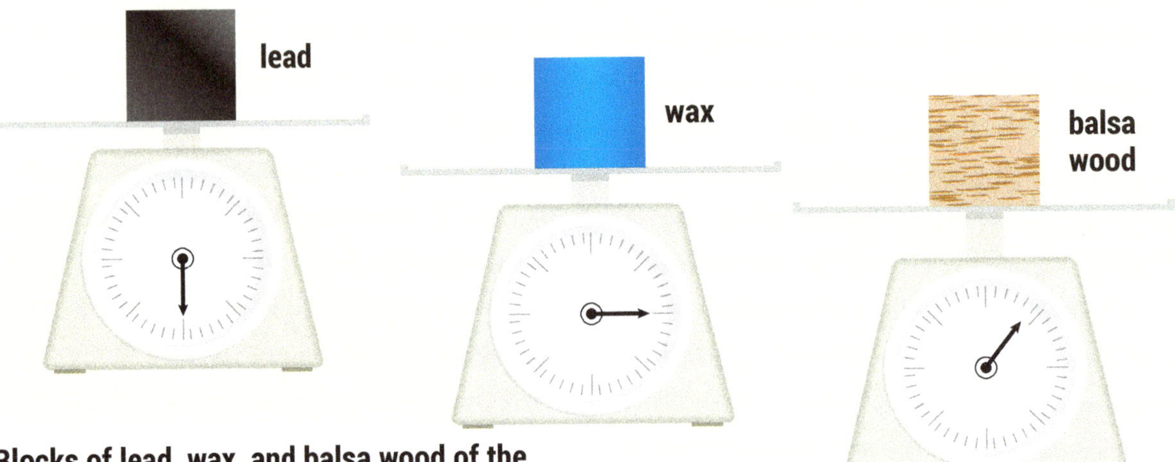

Blocks of lead, wax, and balsa wood of the same size have different weights. The lead is the heaviest. The balsa wood is the lightest.

PACKED TOGETHER

Everything on Earth has density. Density means how dense something is, or how closely its atoms are packed together. Solids are usually more dense than liquids, and liquids are more dense than gases.

Invisible Particles

Everything is made up of tiny invisible particles called atoms. In some materials, the atoms are packed closely together. In other materials, the atoms are farther apart. The atoms in metal are heavier and more tightly packed than those in wood. A piece of metal weighs more than a piece of wood of the same size.

Gold metal has a high density. Bars of gold are very heavy.

FACT

Air has density. Cold air has more density than hot air.

Floating and Sinking

Why do some things float and others sink? It's because of density. Objects that are less dense than water will float. They include plastic bottles and rubber balls. Wood has low density. Objects with higher density than water sink. Things made of metal or stone sink. Metal and stone have higher density than water.

These logs are heavy but will float on water. That's because wood is less dense than the water.

FACT

Oil is less dense than water. If you pour oil into a glass of water, the oil will float. Try it and see!

OIL TANKER

An oil tanker ship is like an empty metal box. It takes up a certain space, or volume. When the ship is loaded with oil, it is much heavier. The volume of the ship does not change, but its mass is bigger. The more oil the tanker carries, the denser it is and the lower it floats in the water. If the tanker's density is less than the density of water, the tanker floats. If its density is more than the density of water, the tanker sinks.

A filled oil tanker weighs more than an empty tanker. It floats lower in the water.

Floating a Boat

When an object is put into water, it pushes some of the water out of the way. The water pushes against the object and may hold it up. A block of metal usually sinks. But if the metal is made into a boat, it will float. A metal ship pushes lots of water away. It also has spaces inside that are filled with air. The ship, including the air, is less dense than water.

Weights Are Useful

We need to weigh things for many reasons. If you're sending a package, you might be asked how much it weighs. Some stores sell food by weight. People need to know how much weight a truck can carry. Or how much weight is too much for a plane to fly.

Following a Recipe

Weights come in handy for cooking. Recipes tell us how to cook things. A recipe is a list of ingredients. It tells us how much of each ingredient we have to use. If we use too much or too little of something, the recipe may turn out wrong.

A cake needs just the right weights of flour, eggs, sugar, and butter to taste good!

Chemistry and Weight

Weights are important in chemistry. Chemistry is the study of materials. Many of the materials we use are made by adding chemicals together. Scientists make new substances by joining chemicals together. Just like a recipe, they weigh the chemicals. They follow instructions on how to mix them.

Scientists have to weigh chemicals accurately.

ELEMENTS

Everything in the universe is made up of elements. There are more than 100 different elements. Some are light and others are heavy. Hydrogen is the lightest element. It is a gas that used to be put inside airships. The heaviest element that exists in nature is a metal called uranium.

Changing Weight

Our weight changes as we get older. As people grow, they get bigger, taller, and heavier. People often weigh themselves by standing on scales.

If you are a certain height and age, you should weigh a certain amount. If you weigh much more than this, you may be overweight. If you weigh much less, you may be underweight. If you eat the right amount of healthy food and get exercise, your weight is probably just right.

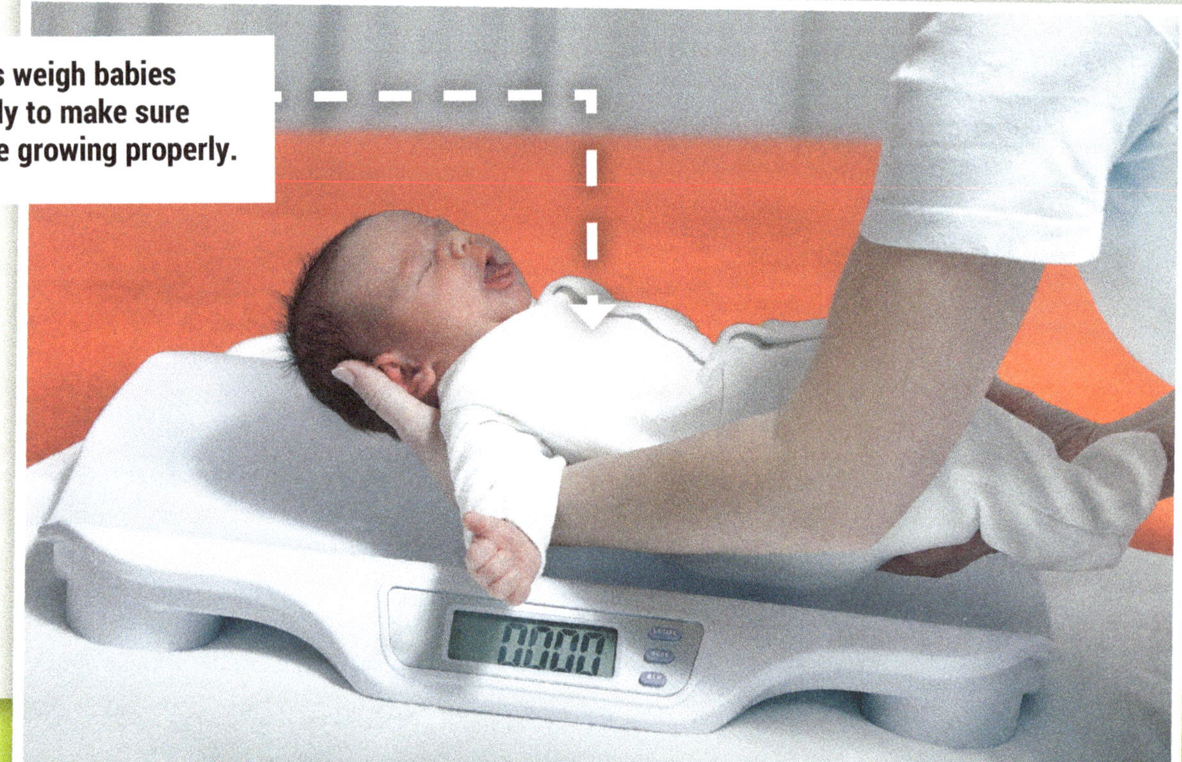

Doctors weigh babies regularly to make sure they are growing properly.

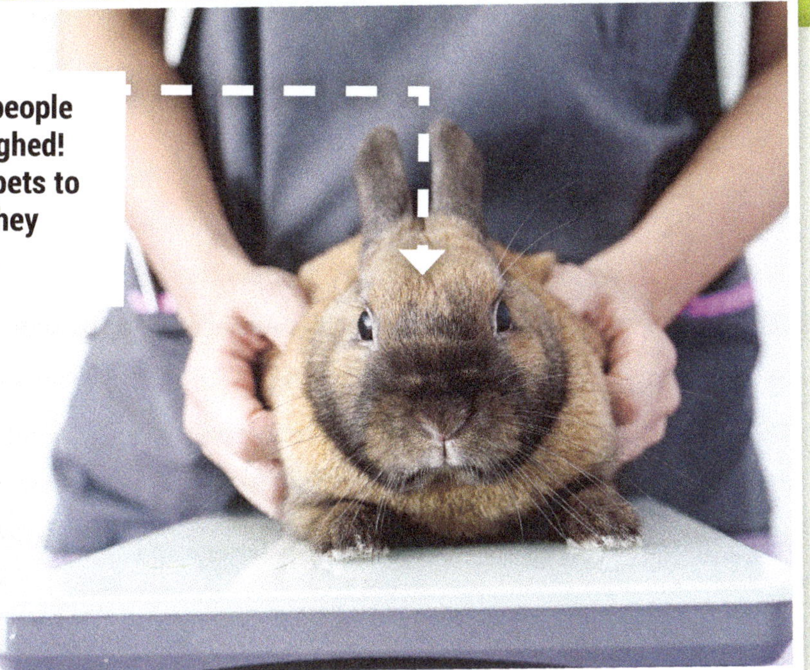

It isn't just people that get weighed! Vets weigh pets to make sure they are healthy.

Healthy Weights

Doctors can sometimes tell if people are healthy or ill by weighing them. If a person has lost a lot of weight, that might mean they are sick. If people have been sick and they start to put weight back on, it might show that they are getting better again.

TRY THIS

Work out the missing weights (pounds or kilograms) where there is a question mark.

Earthworm	5 ounces, or ? grams
Cat	8 pounds, or 3.6 kilograms
Dog	? pounds, or 36 kilograms
Adult human	160 pounds, or ? kilograms
Panda	? pounds, or 136 kilograms
Elephant	7 tons, or 6.3 metric tons

Answers on page 32.

Record Breakers

Animals come in all shapes, sizes, and weights. The heaviest land animal is the African elephant. A full-grown male adult can weigh 6.6 tons (6 tonnes). The blue whale is even bigger. This ocean giant can weigh more than 100 tons (90 tonnes)—as much as 4 to 5 school buses!

The world's heaviest bird is the ostrich. It can weigh over 344 pounds (156 kg). It also lays the biggest eggs in the world—3.1 pounds (1.4 kg).

The African elephant is the heaviest animal on land.

TRY THIS

Ask an adult if you can use the kitchen scales. Collect any vegetables or fruits you have at home. Hold them in your hands. Which feel the heaviest? Now weigh them on the scales.Write down your answers in imperial and metric units. List them with the heaviest first and the lightest last. Were you right?

Pound for pound, leaf cutter ants are some of the strongest animals on the planet. They carry pieces of leaves long distances back to their nests.

Weight Lifters

Some creatures can carry huge weights. An elephant can carry up to 20,000 pounds (9,000 kg) on its back. A leaf-cutter ant can carry 50 times its own weight. And a rhinoceros beetle can carry 850 times its own weight. That is like a person carrying two trucks!

GROWING BIG

It is not just animals that can grow to amazing weights. Around the world, people hold competitions to see how big they can grow vegetables and fruit. In 2021, someone grew a pumpkin that weighed 2,703 pounds (1,226 kilograms). That's about the same weight as 13 adult men!

HANDS ON

Comparing Weights

WHAT YOU NEED

* Weighing scales
* Modeling clay
* Small solid rubber ball
* Empty shoebox
* Large book or some small ones
* Pencil and paper

WHAT YOU DO

1. Make the modeling clay into a round ball the same size as the rubber ball.

2. The two balls have the same volume, but do they have the same weight? Weigh the rubber ball on the scales. Write down how much it weighs.

3. Now weigh the ball of clay. Write down the amount. Is it heavier or lighter than the rubber ball?

This May Help

The balls have different weights but the same volume. The shoebox has the same volume as the books, but it weighs less. Weight is created by gravity. The more mass something has, the greater the force of gravity. The shoebox has less mass and less weight than the books.

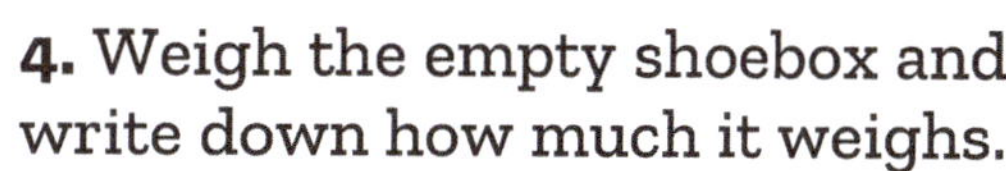

4. Weigh the empty shoebox and write down how much it weighs.

5. Now weigh a small pile of books or one large book that matches the volume of the shoebox. Write down the amount. Which object weighs the most?

Glossary

atom A tiny particle. All matter is made up of atoms.

balance A weighing machine, often with two pans, used with weights.

carat A tiny weight used to weigh precious metals and gems.

density A measure of how much matter something contains.

gram A small unit of weight in the metric system.

gravity The force that pulls things toward Earth.

hundredweight A weight equal to 100 pounds.

imperial The common system of measurement in the United States. Pounds, ounces, inches, and feet are imperial units of measurement.

kilogram A measurement of weight in the metric system.

mass The amount of matter something contains.

matter Anything that has weight and takes up space.

metric A system that measures things in meters and kilograms.

metric ton A large weight equal to 1,000 kilograms.

milligram A tiny weight equal to one-thousandth of a kilogram.

ounce A small weight in the imperial system.

pound A heavier weight than an ounce. There are 16 ounces in a pound.

scales A weighing machine, often with one or two pans, that has a pointer or screen showing the weight.

ton An imperial measurement that weighs 2,000 pounds.

troy A tiny weight used for measuring precious metals and gems.

volume The amount of space something takes up.

weighbridge A huge balance used for weighing cars and trucks.

Find Out More

BOOKS

Askew, Mike.
Let's Measure It. You Can Master Math.
New York: PowerKids Press, 2021.

Celle, Clara.
How Many Llamas Does a Car Weigh?
Mankato, Minn.: Capstone Publishing, 2020.

Dorling Kindersley.
How to Measure Everything.
New York: Dorling Kindersley, 2018.

WEBSITES

www.ducksters.com/science/quiz/mass_and_weight_questions.php
Test your knowledge about mass and weight with this quiz.

www.exploratorium.edu/ronh/weight/
Find how much you would weigh on the moon and different planets!

www.mathsisfun.com/measure/weight-mass.html
Find out the difference between mass and weight, and how we use and measure weights.

Publisher's note to educators and parents: Our editors have carefully reviewed these websites to ensure that they are suitable for students. Many websites change frequently, however, and we cannot guarantee that a site's future contents will continue to meet our high standards of quality and educational value. Be advised that students should be closely supervised whenever they access the Internet.

Index

ANSWERS

Page 11: 3 ounces = 3 x 28 grams = 84 grams; 5 pounds = 5 x 454 grams = 2,270 grams; 6 grams = 6 x 0.04 ounce = 0.24 ounce; 10 kilograms = 10 x 2.2 pounds = 22 pounds. **Page 13:** There are 60 quarters and 20 nickels. **Page 25:** The earthworm is 140 grams; the dog is 80 pounds; the adult human is 72 kilograms; the panda is 300 pounds.